Yellow Umbrella Books are published by Red Brick Learning
7825 Telegraph Road, Bloomington, Minnesota 55438
http://www.redbricklearning.com

Library of Congress Cataloging-in-Publication Data
Cipriano, Jeri S.
    Toys long ago = Juguetes del pasado/by Jeri S. Cipriano.
    p. cm.
    In English and Spanish.
    Summary: "Simple text and photos present the historical aspect of toys"—Provided
by publisher.
    Includes index.
    ISBN-13: 978-0-7368-6023-9 (hardcover)
    ISBN-10: 0-7368-6023-1 (hardcover)
    1. Toys—History—Juvenile literature. I. Title: Juguetes del pasado. II. Title.
GV1218.5.C57 2006
688.7'209—dc22   2005025858

Written by Jeri S. Cipriano
Developed by Raindrop Publishing

Editorial Director: Mary Lindeen
Editor: Jennifer VanVoorst
Photo Researcher: Wanda Winch
Adapted Translations: Gloria Ramos
Spanish Language Consultants: Jesús Cervantes, Anita Constantino
Conversion Assistants: Jenny Marks, Laura Manthe

Photo Credits
Cover: Sandro Vannini/Corbis; Title Page: Huntley Hedworth/Corbis; Page 4: Pocumtuck
Valley Memorial Association, Memorial Hall Museum, Deerfield, MA; Page 6: Pocumtuck
Valley Memorial Association, Memorial Hall Museum, Deerfield, MA; Page 8: Jacqui
Hurst/Corbis; Page 10: Enzo & Paolo Ragazzini/Corbis; Page 12: Photo24/Brand X
Pictures; Page 14: Toy Museum Nuremberg; Page 16: Gary Sundermeyer/Capstone Press

1 2 3 4 5 6 11 10 09 08 07 06

Toys Long Ago

by Jeri S. Cipriano

Juguetes del pasado

por Jeri S. Cipriano

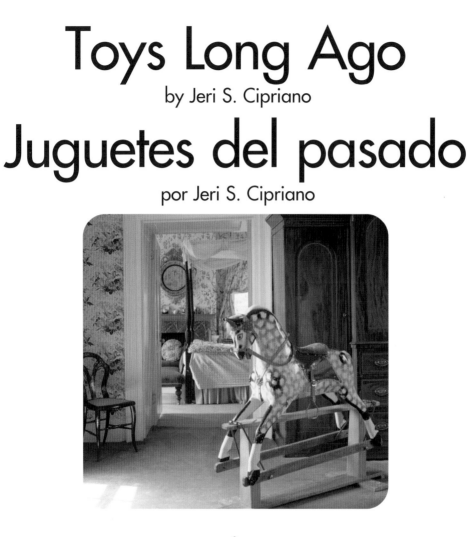

Yellow
Umbrella
Books
for early readers

Long ago, people made
dolls from corn husks.

Hace tiempo se hacían
muñecas de hojas de maíz.

People made dolls
from cloth, too.

Hace tiempo se hacían
muñecas de tela.

Long ago, people made toy horses from wood.

Hace tiempo se hacían caballitos de madera.

Long ago, people made toy cars and trucks from wood.

Hace tiempo se hacían carritos de madera.

Long ago, people made
spinning tops from wood.

Hace tiempo se hacían
trompos de madera.

14

Long ago, people made play figures from tin.

Hace tiempo se hacían soldaditos de plomo.

What is this toy
made from?

¿De qué se hizo
este juguete?

Index

Índice